D1034923

It's Fun to Draw
Farm
Animals

Mark Bergin

**WINDMILL
BOOKS**

New York

Published in 2012 by Windmill Books, LLC
303 Park Avenue South, Suite #1280, New York, NY 10010-3657

Editorial Assistant: Victoria England
U.S. Editor: Jennifer Way

Library of Congress Cataloging-in-Publication Data

Bergin, Mark, 1961-
 Farm animals / by Mark Bergin.
     p. cm. — (It's fun to draw)
 Includes index.
 ISBN 978-1-61533-599-2 (library binding)
1. Domestic animals in art—Juvenile literature. 2. Livestock in art—Juvenile literature. 3. Drawing—Technique—Juvenile literature. I. Title.
 NC783.8.D65B47 2012
 743.6'9—dc23
                                    2011028926

Manufactured in China

CPSIA Compliance Information: Batch #SW2102WM: For Further Information contact Windmill Books, New York, New York at 1-866-478-0556

Contents

Chicken

1 Start with the head. Add a dot for the eye.

2 Add the beak and head details.

3 Add the body.

4 Draw in a wing and tail feathers.

You Can Do It!

Use oil pastels and smudge them with your finger. Use a felt-tip pen for the lines.

Splat-a-Fact

Male chickens are larger and more brightly colored than females.

5 Draw in two legs and feet.

4

Cow

1 start with the head and add two rounded shapes.

2 Add the eyes, nostrils, ears, and horns.

3 Draw the body.

4 Add four legs and hooves.

you Can Do It!

Use crayons for texture and paint over it with watercolors. Use a felt-tip pen for lines.

5 Draw in a tail, an udder, and markings. Add grass.

Splat-a-Fact

No two cows have the same markings or spots.

7

Donkey

1 Draw a bean shape with a dot for the eye.

2 Add nostrils and a mouth.

3 Add ears, a neck, and a mane.

4 Draw a curved body and a tail.

5 Add four legs and hooves.

You Can Do It!

Use a black felt-tip pen for the lines. Add color with colored markers.

8

9

Mallard

You Can Do It!

Use oil pastels and smudge them with your finger. Use a felt-tip pen for the lines.

1 Start with the head. Add a dot for the eye.

2 Draw the beak.

Splat-a-Fact

Ducks have webbed feet that help them swim well.

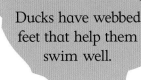

3 Draw in the body with a pointed tail. Add a curved line for the wing and across the chest.

4 Add legs with webbed feet and a zigzag line around the neck.

10

Farm Cat

1 Start by drawing a furry body and head shape.

2 Add an ear, an eye, a nose, and whiskers.

3 Add furry legs and paws. Draw a triangle shape inside the ear.

Splat-a-Fact

Cats have very good night vision.

4 Draw in a bushy tail. Add a striped pattern.

13

Goat

1 Start with the head.

2 Draw in ears, eyes, and a nose.

3 Add horns, a neck, and a beard.

splat-a-Fact
Goats have four stomachs!

4 Draw in the body and tail.

You Can Do It!
Use crayons for all textures. Paint over them with watercolor paints. Use a blue felt-tip for the lines.

5 Add the legs and hooves.

14

Duck

1 Start with the body shape and tail feathers.

2 Add the beak.

3 Draw two webbed feet.

4 Add eyes and a wing. Finish the beak details.

You Can Do It!

Use colored pencils and a felt-tip pen for lines. Color with squiggly lines to add texture.

Horse

1 Start with the head.

2 Add nostrils, a mouth and an eye.

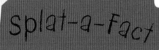

3 Draw in the horse's neck, ears, and mane.

Splat-a-Fact

Horses sleep standing up!

4 Add a bean-shaped body and a tail.

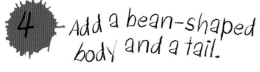

5 Draw in four legs and hooves.

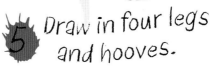

18

Owl

1 Start with the head shape. Add a curved line for detail.

2 Draw in the eyes and a beak.

You Can Do It!
Tear up colored tissue paper and glue it onto white paper for color. Use a felt-tip pen for the lines.

3 Draw the body shape. Add a tail with a fan shape.

4 Add two large, pointed wings.

5 Add two legs and feet.

Splat-a-Fact

Barn owls do not hoot, they screech!

20

21

Pig

You Can Do It!
Color with watercolors. Add ink while the paint is still wet to make an interesting effect.

1 Start with the head. Add an oval for the nose.

2 Add the ears, eyes, nostrils, and a mouth.

3 Add the body.

4 Draw in a curly tail and add spotty markings.

5 Add four legs and feet.

Splat-a-Fact
Some pigs have tusks that they use for fighting and digging.

22

23

Rabbit

1 Start with a circle for the head and an oval for the body.

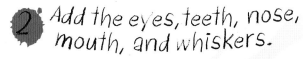

2 Add the eyes, teeth, nose, mouth, and whiskers.

You Can Do It!
Draw the lines with a brown felt-tip pen. Add color with colored pencils.

3 Add four legs.

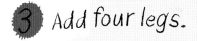

4 Add a tail and ears.

Splat-a-Fact
There are about 25 different species of rabbit.

25

Sheep

A male sheep is called a ram, and a female sheep is called a ewe.

1 Start with a fluffy body.

2 Draw the head shape with a fluffly top and add ears.

3 Add the eyes, mouth, nostrils, and grass.

You Can Do It!
Use watercolor paints to add color. Dab the paint onto the paper with a sponge for texture.

4 Draw four legs and feet. Add the tail.

Sheepdog

Splat-a-Fact
Sheepdogs help farmers to round up sheep.

1 Start by cutting out the shape of the body.

2 Cut out a head. Glue it to the body.

3 Add a tongue. Add eyes and a nose.

You Can Do It!
Cut the shapes from colored paper and glue them into place. The head must overlap the body.

4 Cut out more fur for the head and glue it to your dog.

28

Turkey

You Can Do It!
Use colored pencils.
Put a textured surface
under your paper for
an interesting effect.

1 Start with a curl to make your turkey's body.

2 Add fan-shaped feathers.

3 Draw two legs and spiky feet.

Splat-a-Fact
A baby turkey is called a poult.

4 Draw in a neck and head. Add a beak and an eye. Add head details and zigzags on the tail.

Read More

Berger, Melvin. *Farm Animals*. New York: Scholastic Reference, 2008.

Cooper, Wade. *Farm Animals*. New York: Cartwheel Books, 2009.

Walton, Rick. *Herd of Cows, Flock of Sheep: Adventures in Collective Nouns*. Layton, UT: Gibbs Smith, 2011.

Glossary

groom (GROOM) To clean someone's body and make it neat.

smudge (SMUJ) To blend together.

species (SPEE-sheez) A single kind of living thing. All people are one species.

texture (TEKS-chur) How something feels when you touch it.

whiskers (HWIS-kerz) Hard hairs that grow on a face.

Index

Web Sites

For Web resources related to the subject of this book,
go to: www.windmillbooks.com/weblinks and select this book's title.